Grandma's Attic

Lina Tan
Illustrated by Margaret Power

Emily was helping her grandmother
clean out the attic.

"Look, Grandma,
I've found an old book,"
she said.

"That was my grandmother's diary,"
Grandma said. "She was your
great-great grandmother.
She lived a long time ago!"

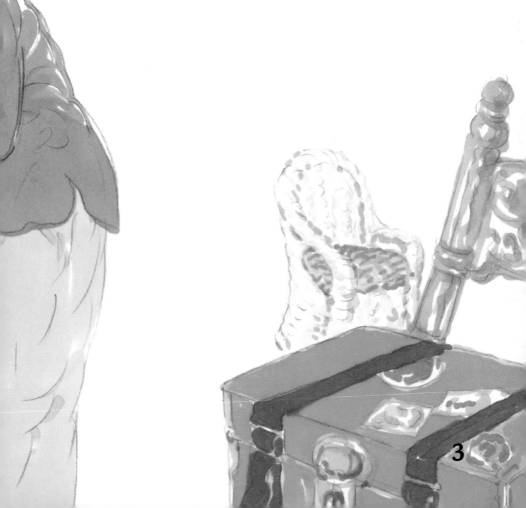

"What was her name?" asked Emily.

Grandma smiled. "Open her diary and find out," she said.

Emily opened the dusty old diary.

"Her name was Emily, too!"
said Emily.

"That's right," said Grandma.
"You were named after your
Great-great Grandma Emily.
She used to write about her life
in that diary."

Our Family Tree

Frank — Emily

Harold — Ethel

Jack — Betty

Jill — John — Kate — Bob

Chad Larry Geri

Emily

"What was she like?" asked Emily.

"Let's find out," said Grandma.

Emily and Grandma turned
the pages of the diary.

9

"Wow! Great-great Grandma Emily
had nice handwriting!" said Emily.

"She wrote everything by hand
when she was young," said Grandma.

"I do most of my writing
on the computer," said Emily.

"Great-great Grandma used to walk two miles each way to school!" said Emily.

"They didn't have many cars
when she was young," said Grandma.

"I take the bus to school," said Emily.
"But I like to take long walks, too."

"Great-great Grandma used to help do the laundry," said Emily.

"That's right," said Grandma.
"She used a bucket and scrub-board
when she was young."

"Wow! I'm glad that we have
a washing machine!" said Emily.

"Look! Great-great Grandma Emily had a pet calf!" said Emily.

"She lived on a farm," said Grandma.
"She helped care for the animals."

"I take care of our pets," said Emily.

17

"Great-great Grandma Emily
knew how to play the piano,"
said Emily.

"She loved music," said Grandma.
"And there were no radios or
CD players when she was young."

"I love music, too," said Emily.

"Great-great Grandma Emily
played checkers," said Emily.

"There was no TV when she was young,"
said Grandma. "We didn't have a TV set
when I was a young girl either!
People played lots of games instead."

"I like playing checkers," said Emily.

"That reminds me," said Grandma. "I have an old checkers game around here somewhere."

"Here it is!" said Emily.
"Let's play!"

"Good idea," said Grandma.

"So many things have changed since your Great-great Grandma Emily's time," said Grandma.

"But some things are still the same!" said Emily with a smile.